I0019380

"Make Money on MySpace"

&

"Resale Rights Profits"

Secrets Revealed

Make Money on MySpace

This small blueprint is about making money on the hot, new, myspace.

I'm not going to add a lot of fluff and filler here, just the downright basics on what you need to do right now to make money on myspace!

The beginning:

Ok, first you need to figure out a few things. There are several ways you can go about creating money for yourself on myspace.

But the easiest way is finding a niche you are interested in, something you know something about that you may be able to help other people with.

But you also need to make sure it is a big enough niche to make money from, and to do that you need to check out the groups and forums on myspace, which are here:

Groups:

http://groups.myspace.com/index.cfm?fuseaction=groups.categories

Forums:

http://forum.myspace.com/index.cfm?fuseaction=messageboard.categories

Now that you have determined that your niche could be profitable, or else have found one that you think will be, you need to register as a member.

First thing you need to do is join myspace here:

http://collect.myspace.com/index.cfm?fuseaction=Join

Now that you are a member, you need to fix up your profile so as to look like an expert in your niche, i.e. focusing on your love or passion for your niche. For this example, I am going to be referring to a dog-training niche. I would write my profile around that, letting people know that I am into dogs and know what I'm talking about when it comes to dogs and to training, and so on.

OK; it asks you to Pick your MySpace Name/URL! Just below where your picture is located, click that link and pick your myspace name/url.

Make sure you pick something related to your niche if possible; so for the dog-training site I will be trying to get a name that has dog training in it. It just so happens I was able to get "mydog_training", so now my new myspace url is:

myspace.com/mydog_training.

So then you need to edit your profile; you need to make it look as good as you possibly can, and add as much detail as possible to your "about me" and "personality" section.

Add a few pictures of you or something related to your niche. Add a layout so as not to use the plain background that myspace gives you, as this is usually what spammers use. You can get free layouts from this place:

http://www.freemyspacelayouts.org/

Or, you can search Google for "free myspace layouts". You can see my myspace profile here: http://www.myspace.com/mydog_training

OK, you have your niche; you got your profile up and looking good -- now you need to find a product to promote. There are several ways to go about this...

You can do affiliate programs or the Google AdSense program, where you get paid per click from putting ads on your site; you can read more about that here:

http://www.internetmarketingcircle.com/advertising/AdSense.html

Any route you go, just make sure it will be worth it. I suggest you sign up for clickbank and promote products from their database of products:

http://www.clickbank.com

You can do several things to promote your product or AdSense site such as jokes, riddles, petitions, and so on, as I will detail more a little bit later, but let's say I'm going to do an AdSense site with an affiliate product on dog training. I will go to groups about dogs, join them and start posting in the forums and message boards. I will only post helpful advice or just brew up some good ol' chats, but I don't advertise; no, I just make friends.

Note: There is a product out called Badder Adder: Add thousands of MySpace friends and automatically send messages, comments, bulletins and event invitations and so on. This is a tool to speed up the adding of friends, but only add about 350 per day to be on the safe side. I'm not saying to get this tool, I'm just telling you that the more friends you have, the quicker you can start the money coming in...

Now once you start posting, you will be getting some friend requests and profile views, so now we add a link to our site or affiliate page in the "about us" section; don't make it blatant, just a smooth way to get people to view it.

While we are building our friend list you will want to create a group about your niche. They make you wait 7 days before you can create a group, so meanwhile we can start to work on our blueprint to make the money.

1ˢᵗ way to make money: Petitions

OK, this one is really simple and is a way to make money daily via AdSense or an affiliate program, and requires about 30 minutes a day. For this one you can make a petition or a survey and have people go and sign it or vote, which ever you choose.

What you need to do once you build your list of friends (I suggest you have at least 800 to 1000 friends) is start posting bulletins. Making it something controversial works best, but it can be anything. So, if it was for my dog niche, I would do something perhaps on pit bulls, i.e. I could do a petition to ban or not ban the pit bulls, such the title could be:

Subject: Help Stop the Pit Bull Breed Ban Petition!

Then I could go on to say in the body:

Body: Aggressive dogs are found among any breed or crossbreed, and breed-specific legislation and breed bans are not effective solutions to the problem of dog attacks; and the problem of dog attacks is best dealt with through a comprehensive program of education, training and legislation encouraging responsible ownership of all breeds, so I pleed that you stop by my petition site and sign it...

Then on the petition page of your site you could have a petition script, which you can find here:

http://www.google.com/search?q=petitionscript&hl=en&lr=&rls=GGLG%2CGGLG%20%3A2005-49%2CGGLG%3Aen

Try to find a good one; here is the one I use and recommend:

http://petitionscript.net/phpPETITION2/index.php

You can then write the petition up and start posting it on your bulletin board and post it to the related bulletins in the groups area of your niche. You can start blogging about it on your myspace blog.

To learn a little about how to write petitions you can view this resource: http://www.petitiononline.com and go through and see how people are writing them up.

Here is another resource:

http://www.google.com/search?result&cd=1&q=how+to+write+a+petition&spell=

This site is where you will add your Google AdSense or affiliate program or the like; it's not uncommon for someone to make $50 to $100 per day if you really study it and spend the time to make it a good petition.

Some more ways to boost the traffic would be to do a press release on the petition, post in related forums about it, or call your local radio or TV station. If it is controversial enough, it will start a viral effect and you won't be able to stop the traffic!

The same steps can be taken for a survey, or voting system as well.

Riddle Me This, Riddle Me That – The 2nd way to make money:

This next tip is a way to make money using riddles, brain scramblers, or jokes.

In this step, you can use the same friends from the petition profile or you can create a new one (I prefer to create a new one), and get members from all walks of life. You don't have to be picky picking these friends, as the market is more broad; I mean, who doesn't like jokes and riddles?!

Do the same in this profile as you did in the last, but make it more fun-based, exciting, and COOL!

You want people to AD you! So make them want to be your friend.

If you use the Badder Adder, you can find a popular profile of someone and start adding their friends; this is the simplest and fastest way to collect friends. And if you use it, add a message so it seems as though you are writing to them personally.

Once you start collecting friends you can start commenting on others' myspace, pictures, and so on; anyway to get your profile in front of a lot of people. Add something that's either controversial or funny so people will send their friends to your profile.

Once you start getting friends, you can post bulletins, and start posting in the group bulletins.

Here is what you can post. This is a riddle I found, but you can use whatever you want:

Three friends check into a motel for the night and the clerk tells them the bill is $30, payable in advance. So, they each pay the clerk $10 and go to their room. A few minutes later, the clerk realizes he has made an error and overcharged the trio by $5.

He asks the bellhop to return $5 to the 3 friends who had just checked in. The bellhop sees this as an opportunity to make $2 as he reasons that the three friends would have a tough time dividing $5 evenly among them; so he decides to tell them that the clerk made a mistake of only $3, giving a dollar back to each of the friends.

He pockets the leftover $2 and goes home for the day! Now, each of the three friends gets a dollar back, thus they each paid $9 for the room which is a total of $27 for the night. We know the bellhop pocketed $2 and adding that to the $27, you get $29, not $30 which was originally spent. Where did the other dollar go????

On your riddle or joke page you can have this text:

"Keep Reading To Find Out How To

Get The Solution To The Missing Dollar

Riddle!"

Then have an AdSense block

You will then suggest to them to add you as a friend, and post the riddle for their

friends to see in their bulletin board…

Also, you can make a code for them to just copy and paste.

Then you can have a link to another page with the solutions.

Here is an example of one I did:

http://myspace.relatingtoall.com/myspaceriddle.html

Feel free to copy this example, or layout.

For this to work really well, you need to make up new riddles, jokes and so forth to keep them going every day, and post them several times a day. Before long you will be making a fair amount of money just from this one tip!

By the way, there are tons of weblog sites out here. One of the most popular ones is Blogger. This is a step-by-step guide to have your blog in Blogger.

"Blueprint   Guide   for   Blogger"
http://ebookuniversal.com/blogblueprint.html

Also, there are a lot of tips for your blog in this book:

"Blog   About   This"
http://ebookuniversal.com/BlogaboutThis.htm

Resale Rights Profits

My real life success story and how I'm working at home as a full time Internet marketer selling products with

Resale Rights

Many ebooks and pieces of software, especially in the field of online or internet marketing, are sold with resell rights included. It is therefore necessary to distinguish between normal resell rights and master resell rights.

Most resale rights packages will not let you alter any of its content or in any way change/tamper with the information. Always read the disclaimers surrounding them. If you wanted to change the content you would have to contact the author and request a partnership or buy the editing rights to the product.

I'm going to briefly share with you my online success story in an endeavor to show you that it is indeed possible for ordinary people (perhaps you) to earn big profits from products with resale rights.

It all began for me back in late 1997. Two things happened at this time that led me to where I am today. The first event was the simple purchase of a computer, and the second event was finding out my wife was pregnant with twins.

I had a very demanding job where I worked long hours and most weekends, so I was faced with the dilemma of knowing that I had no choice other then to spend more time at home to help out with the monumental task of raising twins. (We already had a 3-year-old boy at this stage as well.)

However, the reality was that without working those long hours our income would not be sufficient, and besides my job didn't really give me a choice – working long hours was expected.

As they say. "Necessity is the mother of invention", so I jumped on the computer and searched the Internet for work-at-home ideas. I really didn't have a clue what to look for and in my mind I thought of things like stuffing envelopes.

It was then that I stumbled across a website promoting something called 'paid to surf' programs. It seemed like a good idea to me and so I got involved. Basically, these programs were free to join and in theory you got paid anywhere from .05 cents to .50 cents an hour to allow banner advertising onto your computer.

These programs also had a multi-level payment system built in where you would get paid extra money for every hour someone in your down line watched the ads.

I wasted 18 months or so promoting these programs, and on paper I should be almost a millionaire now from everyone in my down lines. However, reality is that while I did earn a few hundred dollars from them, they basically were a huge failure.

However, something happened while I was promoting those programs.

Even when you fail you succeed...Because you learn so much more by just doing something!

#1. I learned how to create basic web pages. I had no idea how to do this when I first started, and now my web site creating abilities are very good (even if I do say so myself!)

#2. I discovered the importance of email marketing even though I didn't even know it at the time. You see, I just put my email address on my web site asking for those who wanted to know when a new paid-to-surf program was released to join my list.

When a new program came onto the scene (almost daily at one stage), there would be a mad scramble to see who could get the news out first and get all the new sign-ups in their down lines.

This was so simple, yet very effective. I built down lines of hundreds of people this way and this is a concept I will elaborate on more later on in this book for promoting resale rights products.

#3. I also learned how to write and create ebooks. In fact, my first ebook called 'All About Paid To Surf' was pretty good for a beginner.

Now after 18 months of this stuff, I was terribly disappointed when the income was just not coming from them, and one by one, the companies started to fold.

It was then that I decided to pursue those things called Affiliate Programs.

I stumbled and struggled. I was only using programs at Commission Junction (I don't think I even knew the others like Clickbank existed at this stage).

I would pick out an affiliate program and then design an entire set of web pages about it. Finally I started earning good money. I actually started earning $1000 a month from selling mobile phone plans and got so excited I started spending quite a few hundred dollars a month on Pay Per Click advertising.

However, this also fell through with about 80% of the sales being reversed (therefore I was losing most of my commissions). I'd just get an affiliate program earning money and they'd change the rules or the company would close down.

I was actually on the verge of giving up on this Internet marketing stuff altogether. (I didn't even know that what I was doing was Internet marketing!)

I knew I needed my own product to sell and be in control of, however I couldn't think of anything, and I spent many a long hour trying to come up with something.

Somewhere along the line I had joined Terry Dean's NetBreakThrough's membership site and something he said stuck in my mind: You don't have to re-invent the wheel. If you see something working, copy the concept and improve on it.
It was then that I stumbled across products with resale rights.

I purchased a package of books for about $25 and through a set of circumstances I made contact with a great guy named Tom Hua who at that time owned a hot-selling package called Freetosell.

Tom gave me access to this package, which at this time was selling like hot cakes.

However, unlike everyone else, I didn't sell the Freetosell package. I used all of the products from that package and the other package I purchased, and uploaded them individually to my own server.

This created more challenges for me, such as getting my own domain name, working out how to download files and upload them to my server. I didn't have a clue and it was a real struggle working it all out. This book will show you how to do all of those tasks.

I then created a sales page and my first resale rights site was in business. I called it the ebookresellerkit. I then started advertising at Overture and instantly

I was making a lot of sales.

The amazing thing about being in the resale rights business is that just by being involved, ideas then started to flow. Where once I would rack my brain and try to think of an idea to write about, now I've got too many. I have written quite a few ebooks now and I can honestly say that the resale rights business got me going.

The old ebookresellerkit site doesn't do much these days as I don't promote it at all. I have since moved on to my latest resale rights business, Reprint Rights Marketing, where again I've added a few extra twists, including free access to a big training site called InfoProduct Marketing.

I mention these things to you to both show you the evolution of my success and also to point out that my success comes from being different – it is important that you just don't follow the pack.

If you see something that works, copy the concept – IMPROVE on it and add your own unique twist to it.

Also, I'm an ordinary guy with no educational qualifications to speak of and no sales background at all; so the old saying rings true: If I can do it, anyone can do it.

I sincerely hope this book proves to be very beneficial to you.

Reprint Rights Marketing

http://www.reprint-rights-marketing.com/

Hey it's my book, so I can list my site first, okay? ☺

The types of resale rights products available from my site are what I call generic. Therefore whoever owns the product also has the resale rights to the product as well.

The advantages are that you get lots of products to sell. In fact, this site will supply you with every master resale rights product that comes onto the market that is allowed to be included in membership sites.

Another advantage is free access to the huge training area including a myriad of top quality ebooks covering most Internet marketing subjects. Disadvantages are that the resale rights products are generic and there is a lot of competition.

Pushbutton Publishing

Bryan Winters Pushbutton Publishing resale rights membership provides an excellent opportunity for anyone who is interested in starting a resale rights business.

Bryan gives you instant access to thousands of dollars worth of resale rights products ready for you to resell and keep 100% of the profits. Bryan Winters also buys every new resale rights product that comes onto the market so that his members always have fresh products to sell.

Pushbutton Publishing also supplies free of charge such essential services as web hosting, autoresponders, ad tracking and more...

Reprint Rights Every Month

Louis Allport's Reprint Rights Monthly membership site over-delivers. Louis Allport has a very unique resell rights club. His ebooks are of standout quality.

Membership to his exclusive reprint rights site gives you rebrand rights to every ebook, and his products include ready-to-go sales pages, audio and excellent Internet marketing tutorials.

The tools Louis provides inside his members area are great, including step-by-step instructions, video tutorials and a marketing forum where he answers questions very quickly.

This resell rights site is one of the best ones out there and with the careful guiding hand of Louis Allport you are guaranteed to do well.

EbookWholesalers

Tom Hua, who it could be said started the resale rights packaging craze with his famous Freetosell package, raised the bar for resale rights marketing when he produced ebookwholesalers.

This exclusive resell rights club is top-class. You get 2 brand new ebooks with resell rights every month and the resale rights can only be obtained from ebookwholesalers.

Some great resell rights ebooks which are written on a wide variety of subjects, plus an excellent community discussion board and top-class support service make this resell rights club a premium service.

Ebookwholesalers continues to grow and expand, and is a fantastic resell rights club to belong to. It is owned by someone who has been in the resale rights business for a long time, plus Tom has joint ventures with quality support teams including Teresa King. You are in very capable hands, and ebookwholesalers comes with the highest possible recommendation.

ProfitsVaultMonthly

Jimmy Brown is a very successful Internet marketer and his ProfitsVaultMonthly resale rights membership site is a real gem.

This is an exclusive membership with ebook products that are written on subjects that actually teach you the Internet marketing business. So not only are Jimmy Brown's ebooks profitable to resell, they are very educational as well.

Jimmy provides you with everything you need including web sales pages. This site also comes with a very impressive affiliate program and is a must-join resale rights club. I'm in the fortunate position of now being familiar with most ebooks and authors these days. But even now - sometimes I have to investigate further to make sure. This is one of the benefits of buying from someone you can trust. And I don't know about you, but I would even be willing to pay an expert more money for peace of mind then to pay a bargain basement price to some sleazy operator who is going to get me in trouble.

This can relate to a lot of things you buy so... Beware of whom you buy from!

There are a lot of resell rights products available from online Auctions, however this is one place you need to be extra careful. So many illegal sellers are auctioning products they have no rights to.

There ARE good bargains to be made; just make sure you do your homework before purchasing.

Sometimes doing a simple search on Google for the product being sold will reveal whether it is legitimately being sold with resell rights or not.

WEB HOSTS

This is a necessary expense for this business. Do not use a free web host! For the ebook business, you must leave yourself with plenty of room to grow, as you will be acquiring more and more books all the time...

I use Host4Profit - for me they have been great. This isn't to say they are the only one to use. There are now many, very good web-host providers.

However, I can only speak from my own experience. Host4Profit provide me with the 3 most vital ingredients:

1.

    300 megs of web space, which is ideal   for hosting all of my ebooks.

2.

10 gig of data transfer (traffic), which is very generous. This allows me to get plenty of traffic to my site and also accommodates all of the ebooks being downloaded by hundreds of people.

3.

The ability to install your own cgi scripts. This is very important. Many of the modern day scripts can be installed on your own server, which give you a lot of options, especially for automating your business.

As I said before, there are many high-quality web-hosting providers to choose from, however for me Host4Profit have been very reliable.

It should be noted that if you are a member of Pushbutton Publishing or EbookWholeSalers, you can use the web-hosting service they provide.

SETTING UP A DOMAIN

It took me by surprise when many of my newsletter subscribers had no idea how to set up a domain. Of course, it shouldn't have because it was only a few years back that I was hopelessly frustrated by it all as well.

So here is a simple, step-by-step tutorial for you....

Step 1.

Finding a domain name. I believe the actual domain name these days are of minimal importance for your search engine rankings. So try to find a domain name that will be easy to relate with your business.

I use orderyourdomains.com to register my domains. This doesn't mean they're the best, it just so happens I use them and I'm very satisfied with their customer service.

So when you go to any domain registration service, the first thing you'll need to do is search to see if the domain name you want is available.

Step 2.

After hitting the go button you're taken to the next screen where to my surprise this domain name was taken.

At this point, you can perform a whois lookup to see who actually owns the domain, or continue searching for an available domain name... We continue searching.

Step 3.

After clicking go for the next search... if your domain name is available you are taken to the next screen...

You then just click on the checkout button and follow the instructions in order to pay for your new domain. That's it - you own it.

But your work's not over yet, as you need to change the DNS settings of your domain name to point toward your web host. This is the only way to get your web site live.

Step 4.

So you log into your account.

Step 5.

Click on the Change DNS/Hosting Info link

Step 6.

Then select which domain name you want to change the DNS information for and click continue.

Step 7.

You then enter the DNS information in the box above for your web host, and click on save and the job is done. It will take between 24-48 hours for your new domain name to start working.

Wondering where you get the DNS/Hosting information?

When you first sign up with your web host, they send you an email with your login details and other hosting details; however, they also include your DNS/Hosting information.

Well, there you have it. You just copy and paste the above DNS information into your domain manager account. While I've used orderyourdomains in the tutorial above, it will be very similar with every domain registrar.

CREDIT CARD PAYMENTS

To be quite frank, if you cannot accept credit card payments, you're wasting your time. If you just rely on checks and money orders you will miss out on the majority of your sales. I recommend four third-party credit card providers. These are the cheapest options for you to get started and will save you wasting money on unnecessary merchant accounts.

1. Clickbank

I rate Clickbank #1 solely on their ease of use combined with the ready, in-built affiliate program. Download our book Working With Clickbank for a step-by-step tutorial.

2. 2 Checkout.com

I also use this company and I am very pleased with them. However if you want an affiliate program, you will need to set up your own.

3. PayPal

A very popular payment processor and free to set up. This may be your best option when first starting out. I also believe strongly in offering Paypal as a secondary payment alternative for all of your products.

4. Paysystems

These guys are now my primary payment processor and I couldn't be happier with their service.

Paypal provides a great and very affordable way for you to accept payments online. However, there is one major drawback and that is that when you use the order buttons that Paypal provides, and you want to give your customers direct access to their product after purchase - thieves can right click on your webpage and view source and see your thankyou page.

They can then get your product without paying.

However, Paylock Pro, which you get as a free bonus with this ebook, goes a long way to solving the problem by encrypting the Paypal payment links.

SEQUENTIAL AUTORESPONDERS

In this next tutorial, I'm going to show you how easy it is to use one of the Internet marketer's most valuable tools -- the sequential autoresponder.

What is a sequential autoresponder?

It allows you to send pre-written messages to your list at any time-interval you want. For example, message 1 will go out immediately, and then you can set message 2 to go out the next day, or in 3 days time, or even in a year's time. Same goes for every message you have - you can set it to go out at anytime that you wish.

Another way of using this tool is for your newsletter. Say you are going on holidays. A good sequential autoresponder system will even allow you to set the date you want certain messages to go out on. So, you could pre-write your newsletter and have it set up to go out for 4 weeks without you even being there.

I use my easyautopro system, however all decent sequential autoresponder systems will be very similar to set up.

AD TRACKING

Modern technology can sometimes be a frustrating thing to keep up with, however when it comes to ad tracking, what can be done now is marvelous.

If you do any sort of advertising, you must track your ad results or you might as well just throw your money away...

It is easy to set up ad trackers with my easyautopro system.

Please note that the set up procedure for all of the decent ad tracking services will be very similar.

Do you have more then one order-link on your web site?

If so, you can use a different tracking url for each one to see which link is producing the most sales.

Do you have a pop-up on your site? Use ad

tracking links for all of the url's on your pop-up to see which ones people are interested in the most.

Are you seeing the power of ad trackers? Use them to test virtually any link you have either on your web site or in advertising and you'll soon see a trend developing which will tell you where you need to focus most of your energy and where you need to change.

HOW TO DOWNLOAD EBOOKS

There are 2 types of ebooks.

Those that come in .exe format, which do not work on Mac computers, or PDF files which work on all computers.

To read PDF files you'll need The Free Acrobat Reader or the full version of Acrobat, version 3 or higher.

You can download the Free Reader from

Adobe at:

http://www.adobe.com/products/acrobat/readstep.html

To save the PDF and .EXE ebooks to your computer, simply click on the right mouse button over the ebook links. Then click on either "Save Link As" in Netscape or "Save Target As" in Explorer. If you click on the left mouse button the EXE books will download fine, however the PDF books will just open from your server and will not be saved to your computer.

Once you select "save target as" or "save link as", a download screen will come up asking you where you want to save the file to on your computer.

Find the folder you'd like to save the files in and then click on "Save." When you have finished downloading the ebook, just go to the folder you downloaded the file to and double click to open and read.

EDITING

I've been involved in the resale rights industry now for a very long time, and one of the most annoying and frustrating things has always been the labor-intensive job of editing all of the details on those ready-to-use web pages.

But not any more...

One of the products you can download as a bonus with this package (and indeed comes with resell rights) is called Easy Resell Plus. With this software you can edit those pesky links with a click of a button.

THANK YOU PAGES

In our previous article, we found a way around one of my biggest bug-bears which is editing web sites. Well, the next biggest pain is creating thankyou pages for every product I have.

The Easy Reseller Plus package provided the answer for the first problem, and it solves this second problem as well, with the Easy Thankyou Page Creator that you can get inside the Easy Resell Plus software.

With the easyautopro system it is also very easy to set up thankyou pages for product delivery. Plus you have the added advantage of digital download protection because the download link for each customer automatically expires after 24 hours.

To set up, you just go into the Delivery section and fill in the details.

1 Type in (or copy and paste) the product download URL

2Type in any download instructions you wish to include

3Type in the text you want displayed for the download link

UPLOADING FILES TO YOUR WEB SITE

This example of uploading files is with an FTP program that is called Coffee Cup; however it should be very similar to other FTP programs.

1 Start the FTP program and then click on file and then on add new server.

2 Enter a name to describe the site. This will be for your reference only. For this demo I am using the reference 'test'.

3 Enter your username and password. Your web host provider would have given these to you when you signed up.

4 Enter your web site address and the folder where your pages will go.

5I just leave this set at no - if you have a proxy server, click yes and follow the instructions.

6 Click the finish button. You have just set up your web site profile - you will not have to do these steps again.

7 Now you can upload your files. First click on the connect button and then choose which web site you want to upload too. In this case, I am using test so I double click on test.

8 You are then presented with 2 screens. On the left are the files on your computer and on the right are the files on your web server.

9Now all you have to do is upload your files. Choose which files you want to load - in this example I am uploading the instant ebook business web site - by selecting a file and holding the shift key and scrolling down to the bottom file. All files are highlighted - so you can upload more than 1 file.

You then click the right mouse button and choose upload and the files will be uploaded to your web site.

BUILDING A HIGHLY TARGETED MAILING LIST

Earlier in this book, I told you the story of my early days online and how I simply built a list with the sole purpose of notifying them of when a new 'Paid to Surf' program was available.

This same simple tactic will work within the resale rights market as well.

You see, what you might not realize is that there are a consistent number of people who continually buy these products. There is a ready market.

Now, if you can build a list that consists purely of resale rights enthusiasts, then you have a real winner and it is very easy to do.

Then every time you acquire a new product, simply

notify your list immediately that there is a new product available – you will be amazed at how many sales you make!!

IMPORTANT: Don't do anything else with this list. I really mean this... Don't send them newsletters, don't send them any other promotional material, no matter how tempting it is to do so – just contact them when a new resale rights product is ready.

This way they will know that when you send an email it will have what they are interested in and you will make big profits. BUT if you start sending all sorts of different mailings your profits will eventually fade away.

To set up an email capture form or pop-up is very easy to do. If you belong to any autoresponder service they will have instructions explaining how it is done.

If you want to create a pop-up, then use the bonus product that comes with this package called 'Create Your Own Pop Ups in 2.5 Minutes'.

Don't be deceived by the simplicity of what I've just told you. It will work!

SUBMIT YOUR SITE TO THE SEARCH ENGINES

This is a huge subject all of itself, however needless to say this is the first step in your promotional efforts.

So, step 1, submit your site to the search engines and then get on with your life with all of the other promotional methods because it can take anywhere from a few weeks to 2 months to get listed.

The following site has lots of valuable free information about submitting your site, so if you are totally new to this concept, I highly recommend you spend some time going over this information.

http://searchenginewatch.com/webmasters/index.php

One search engine marketing ploy I have not seen anyone use in the resale rights industry (doesn't mean someone's not doing it) is to write search engine friendly articles about the ebooks or software you are selling.

For example, I have a product called Instant Cover Graphics. I could write an article page explaining the importance of creating ebook covers, how they increase conversion rates, how people judge a book by its cover and so forth.

I could then introduce the above package or any other related packages I have and weave references to them from within the article.

I could also join affiliate programs to related products such as ECover Generator.

This will give you a much better chance of attracting free search engine traffic as well as give you a very impressive web site for visitors to come back to.

Plus the affiliate programs will give you a second bite of the cherry. If you can't sell your product, you can still make commission from the affiliate program.

You can take this one step further by writing reviews about each product you have as well.

These methods will bring in great results over time if you're willing to put in the work.

CREATING A SIGNATURE FILE

It's sometimes amazing to me how the easiest marketing tactic of them all is quite often never used - especially by newbies.

I'm talking about a signature file. A signature file goes on the bottom of every email you send out, every article you write, and on every forum message you post. So let's look at how it's done.

The email signature file is very easy to create. This example is using MS Outlook, but it won't be all that much different with other email software. Go to tools, click on options, and then on signatures.

You can create as many sig files as you want. Select the signature file to use as your default and click on the box to use your sig file on all outgoing email.

And that's it. You will need to TEST your sig file just as you would with any other marketing method you use. TEST different headlines, etc. It's your own classified ad wherever you go.

The same principle is to be used on all your articles you write. Something I think you should add to your sig file (and so should I) is a link to your autoresponder ecourse.

Next, use the same principle when contributing to online forums. As in Tony Blakes forum, most forums have a similar form whereby you can fill in the details for your sig file.

This leaves a link that people can click on and check out your site plus it provides an extra link to your site that the search engines like.

Make sure you strictly follow forum etiquette.

Therefore no spam or blatant advertising is allowed. Only post when you have a question and need advice, or when you can contribute by helping someone else with an answer.

Your sig file will do all the advertising you need.

HOW TO ADVERTISE ON PAY PER CLICK ENGINES

As I mentioned earlier – when I first started out I made lots of sales using PPC search engines. However, I believe the competition has gotten tougher and it's now harder to make big profits from PPC search engines for resale rights products. That doesn't mean it can't be done.

One tactic, if using the generic search terms of resale rights, resell rights and reprint rights, is to use a link in your advertising that points to an ad tracker of some sort.

Then, from within your ad tracking software, you can change where that link points to without ever having to change the URL you have listed with the PPC search engines.

The idea is to always point that URL to the latest package that has been released. You should be aware that the words mentioned above can become quite expensive and your sales conversion rate may not justify the expense.

You will ALWAYS show more profit by drilling right down to specific key word phrases. Use keywords that describe what you are selling.

Or use the actual name of the product.

You will make more profit this way, however it will be slow unless you have hundreds of campaigns, as there will not be as much traffic coming to your site for such phrases. However if you use general phrases you will get a lot of traffic but lose money anyway.

SUCCESSFUL CASE STUDY NUMBER ONE: HOW TO PROFIT FROM RESALE RIGHTS

I'm going to show you how successful marketer Jimmy Brown is using resale rights.

Go ahead and click on his name above and have a look at his site. The first thing you are greeted by is a pop-up asking you to subscribe to his free ecourse.

This is marketing tactic number 1.

What's the big deal you ask?

Jimmy has this invitation to join his ecourse inside every ebook he sells.

Think about this now. This ecourse has links to various products that Jimmy sells AND invites you to join HIS affiliate program.

So not only does he immediately earn income from

the links within the books, he also gets to build a huge list of highly qualified people who he will also earn an income from. And he is growing his affiliate base where he has more people promoting his products, that in turn give away or sell his books...and we're back full circle.

Marketing tactic number 2:

Jimmy offers FREE ebooks. You will see a link at the top of the page that takes you to a sales letter (YES - you still have to sell people to take your free offer) that invites you to rebrand the books with your affiliate link for Jimmy's products.

This encourages you to give away these books so you can make commissions. But guess what?

Not only is Jimmy making extra sales because of the spread of these books, he is gaining more subscribers to his list because every book invites people to join his free ecourse.

This is viral marketing at its best, folks!

But wait, there's more...

Jimmy also offers products with generic resale rights (therefore whoever owns the product can resell the product).

Yet again, inside every one of these books people are invited to join his free ecourse. So because you own the resale rights and can make a profit from selling the books, you are going to be real keen to sell as many books as you can.

Then the people you sell to will be the same and so on. And all the time Jimmy is getting new subscribers to HIS list.

This is truly so SIMPLE and I truly hope you can see the enormous viral marketing power of this.

BUT...

Yes, there's more...

I titled this article "The best way to profit from resell rights".

If you look at some of Jimmy's products, they don't all come with resale rights.

For example, if you click on the link that says 'Ebook Power Tools' you are taken to a sales page for that product. Now scroll down to the bottom and you will see a table with the following statement:

If You Would Like Information on Purchasing a Reprint Rights License to eBook Power Tools package Click Here

When you click through to the page, you will see Jimmy is offering resell rights for $247.00

Also, read through Jimmy's license agreement and I also believe this is the best way to do it.

Quite frankly, I believe this is the most profitable way to profit from resale rights.

If you create your own product, offer a limited resale rights license for a further fee. Most of Jimmy's products have a fee of $97 for the license.

Now think about it.

Every person who buys those rights is out there selling the product, and inside that product people have the opportunity to buy the rights ONLY from Jimmy.

He has control and he has the chance to earn big

money.

Don't overlook the power of this. As momentum builds and you get quite a few products out there, then those $97.00 payments are going to start coming in on a regular basis.

As far as I am concerned, this is the best model to base a resale rights business on.

And Jimmy is using EVERY smart viral marketing tactic.

1He gets people to subscribe to his lists and gets free advertising from other people giving away or reselling his books.

2He is earning front-end income from selling the books and the resell rights from his sales page.

3He is earning back-end income from inside the books (once again from free advertising when others sell the books) when people decide they want to purchase the resale rights.

By only making the rights directly available from him, he also is remaining in control of the product.

If you have the ability to write your own ebooks, then this is the system of selling that I recommend you follow.

SUCCESSFUL CASE STUDY NUMBER TWO: ADD A UNIQUE TWIST

I'm constantly harping at anyone who will listen, that to be successful online you must do something that makes you different from the pack.

And once again, it doesn't have to be a huge difference and the best way to explain it to you is to show you how someone has done it.

Well, over a year ago Eva Almeida purchased my Achieving Lift Off ebook for $27.

Inside that book was a bonus package that I created called the All About Ebooks Package which sold for $34.95. You can still see this package here...

Now over the last year or so, when searching Google for resale rights products, I've noticed Eva consistently advertising this package and thought to myself she must be doing okay with it.

Now, I myself did nothing with this package after I created it, and I dare say thousands of people now have this same package because of the Achieving Lift Off book.

But NO ONE except Eva has been smart enough to do something with it.

I noticed over time that she created new ebook covers for the sales page and then by accident I stumbled across the BIG change Eva has introduced just recently to this very same package. (Talk about getting great mileage out of the same product!)

Now she has added video tutorials to the package and this has really made her stand out from the crowd.

You can see it here...

 http://www.ebookresellerkit.com/basics.html

Notice the difference from the old original above.

I myself have been so busy with so many projects, I've neglected many of my former web sites. My old http://www.ebookresellerkit.com has been left alone and sales have virtually dried up.

However for another example for you, go there now and have a look at how I've once again tried to be different from everyone else while using many of the same products.

(Please note I paid Eva $197 for the rights to resell those videos). I'm not happy with the sales page yet, but at least it's a start.

The point to all of this is that you need to do something that's a little different from everyone else. In this case Eva (or her partner with this site) has used a program called Camtasia to create instructional videos.

In fact, I now use Camtasia quite often.

This can be done with ANY product or package you have.

Hopefully, this example will help you think outside of the box and no matter how much competition there is, if you differentiate yourself enough, you still can succeed online.

SUCCESSFUL CASE STUDY NUMBER THREE: INSTANT TURNKEY PACKAGING

This is a very common way people make money from resale rights. Simply compile a number of products into one ebook or software application.

I'm going to show you three examples of this.

Instant Ebook Business

I created this package and added my own unique twists to it.

As you can see, all the products are available from just one ebook. I created the ebook with some basic tutorials and also included some recommended resources so I can earn money on the back-end from affiliate programs.

I also do most of the work with this one, as customers don't have download all the products – just one book and web page. Their customers can download everything from within the book.

Once again I'm trying to get you to think of unique

ways to promote resale rights products. In fact, if you create a package and come up with a killer sales letter, you may have people like me buy the package just for the sales letter (because we already own most of the products).

The Ultimate eBusiness

This is very similar to the above product and is a very good seller.

The original creator of this package, Len Thummond, also provides another unique twist by providing the opportunity for you to purchase a CD containing all of the products.

RABDigital

This is another example of a compilation of products, only this one comes in the form of a software application. It is advertised as One Application with over 165 resellable products.

This is just a small sample of how you can be more creative and unique when selling products with resale rights.

SUCCESSFUL CASE STUDY NUMBER FOUR: DOES THAT ITEM BEING SOLD ON EBAY LOOK FAMILIAR?

While cruising Ebay one night, I found an auction which really caught my eye for two reasons.

I titled this article - 'Does that item look familiar?'... Well, it did! You see, this auction was selling the exact same web templates available over at reprint-rights-marketing.com

BUT -- Unlike 99% of others trying to sell these templates, this person has designed a ready to go web site / business that looks way more appealing.

So much so, that the opening bid is set for $99 and the buy-it-now option at $895.80 - WOW - that's a big profit and it will be interesting to see how much it finally goes for.

Update: This item eventually sold for $128.45, plus they earned a further $5.00 a month for web hosting on the back-end.

So I ask the question... You can have the exact same product to sell if you want to - can you create a web site and a follow-up system as well?

Of course, you might be happy just to create similar sites and sell them on ebay, however I'm thinking you could create such a site and earn a regular income from affiliate programs.

Either way, it shows what you can do by being a little different.

UPSELLING

If I were to tell you that I could improve your profits by 33% almost instantly, for very little effort, would you be interested?

Then listen up – because I'm about to show you exactly how easy it is – and it's called upselling.

The chances are, if you're like most people in business, you aren't utilizing the power of upselling to its greatest effect, and in real dollar terms I'm talking about at least another 33% in profits and indeed as much as 50% in some circumstances.

First of all, what is upselling?

I think it is easier to explain by showing you some examples – so let's have a look at some examples.

1. MacDonalds

MacDonalds and indeed just about any other fast food chain are excellent at upselling. How many times have you heard...

Would you like fries with that? Or, would you like a dessert with that?

Or what about their meal deals? Regular, medium or large!

Most people go for the large...These examples, my friend, are called upsells.

Every time someone places an order they are asked if they want something extra, be it a drink, fries, dessert and so on. Now, what if only 10% of the customers actually responded to the upsell and spent just an extra $2.00?

With the millions of people passing through the doors, this would add up to millions of dollars in extra profits every week.

Now when we start talking about upselling, some business people think they couldn't possibly ask their customers for extra money – it would be too rude.

However have you ever been offended at MacDonald's when asked if would you like fries with that?

Of course not… In fact, in most cases an upsell is actually helping your customer, as we will see in the following example…

2. Garden Center

I read a story about certain business people feeling too awkward about upselling and one such person was operating a gardening center. People would come in and purchase certain plants for the garden and then they'd leave without the owner ever trying to upsell.

That is, until the day it was actually pointed out to them that they were doing the customers a disservice by not doing so. You see, the owner had great knowledge about those plants and knew that they grow better with certain fertilizers and in certain soils.

Why not upsell the fertilizer and/or the soil? After all – do you want your customers to have their plants die? Presumably not – but that's exactly what will happen without the expert advice which of course leads to an upsell anyway.

So this Garden Center owner tried upselling and was astounded at both the huge increases in profits and in customer satisfaction as well. So do you see how easy it is to upsell?

When selling plants you have fertilizer, soil, pesticides, fancy pots and so on; many ways to increase your profits.

Let's look at a few more examples…

3. Dell Computers

I recently purchased a laptop computer online from Dell and here is my experience.

I wanted a Dell computer because of their reputation and service (another lesson on marketing here with name branding). Anyway, I went to their home site and found a nice laptop on special for $2600 AUD and thought, you beauty, I'll get that.

So I click on the purchase button only to be greeted by many more options. This was upselling.

Before I went to the checkout I could add more memory, get a different monitor, a surge protector, and even a fancy leather carry-case. At the end of the day, I spent $3000 AUD on my new laptop. I opted for extra memory, a surge protector and a carry case.

But do you see the bottom line here? Dell got an extra $400.00 out of me – all from upselling. And I could have spent much more!

How much extra money do you think Dell is making from this? I would suspect that in this case almost everyone would spend a little extra money, and as such, Dell is doing extremely well from this.

Now I believe that in every case I've examined so far, anyone not in business wouldn't have a clue what an upsell is. In fact, some people in business don't even know what it is. It's just a better way of running your business and offering your customers more choices.

BUT – it is a brilliant way to increase your profits when running your own
business.

Let's look at another example…

4. Amazon

I quite often purchase books from Amazon and they too are very good at upselling.

When you select a book to purchase, they present you with a message that says people who purchased this book also purchased the following books.

So you as a customer can instantly see similar books about the subject you are interested in, and Amazon as a business gets the chance to double or triple their profits from upselling.

Okay... So how can you apply this to your business?

Again, let's look at some examples...

I was selling an ebook about ebay. It came with a very good salesletter and had a good conversion rate selling at $24.95.

What I did was gather all of the other ebooks I had that were about ebay auction selling. I then wrote an upsell offer on the order page. I didn't even get fancy with it – I just offered all of the extra products for just $15 more.

From the people who purchased, a whopping 45% bought the dearer package. In real dollar terms, for every 100 packages sold, 45 paid the extra $15.

Therefore I earned an extra $675 per 100 customers for just a few minutes work.

I again ask a question…

How happy would you be if you could get an extra $15 out of every product you own? All you have to do to get it is introduce the UPSELL.

Let's look at yet another example….

I know of a membership site that has a silver membership and a gold membership.

The sales letter is brilliant. It throws everything at you so you can't wait to join. But when you click to order, you are taken to another page where you're offered silver or gold membership. Only this time, the wording is slanted heavily in favor of the more expensive gold membership. In fact, it almost makes the silver membership sound like a waste of money.

Remember, the sales letter already had you convinced you wanted membership; you were already happy with silver, yet now that you've seen the gold membership, human nature being what it is, you fear that if you don't take the gold membership you'll be missing out on something.

So what happens?

50% or more people go for the gold membership, which is an extra $10 per month.

That is a brilliant upsell.

I've seen this same tactic with ebook packages. The customers click through to order and then have to decide if they want to spend just a little bit more for the gold package.

So how can you maximize upselling for yourself?

#1. Utilize your autoresponder messages better.

With every product I now sell I use a similar follow-up message to the following:

Hi firstname,

Thank you for your purchase. If modern technology has behaved itself you should have already been automatically re-directed to the download instructions and hopefully already have 33 Days to Online Profits sitting on your computer.

Just in case something went amiss, here are the download details again... You can download the product by clicking here

People who purchased 33 Days to Online Profits also purchased the following products...

Marketing Brain Dump - "Can You Answer The 52 Most Important Questions About Internet Marketing?"

7 Simple Steps to Unlimited Profits - Here's How to Generate an Avalanche of Profits by Using A Simple, Step-by-Step System to Creating and Selling Your Own Products on the Net!

Other Recommended Products and Services...

Reprint Rights Marketing - I'll Buy EVERY Newly Released Resale Rights Product For You With My Own Money and Provide You With The Tools, Training and Services You Need As Well!

EasyAutoPro - How you can avoid lost sales, embarrassing ordering mistakes, incompatible and expensive ecommerce software, and increase sales and customer loyalty...

Reprint Rights Marketing - I got this idea from Steve Pierce in one of his follow-up emails after purchasing his ebook, The Whole Truth

Basically, this is using the Amazon style of upselling. I let my customer know of similar products and other recommended resources.

#2. Utilize your order page better.

Here is my old upsell page for ebay package I mentioned earlier. There's nothing stopping you from doing something similar...

Upsell Sample

#3. Utilize your actual sales page better.

Below is an example of 3 different ordering options. Scroll down towards the bottom of the page and see the 3 different options. This is similar to MacDonalds' small, medium or large.

http://www.instantebookbusiness.com/minisites/index.html

There are many, many ways you can introduce an upsell to your business. What you have seen so far are just a few small examples. I'm sure you can come up with plenty of ideas of your own, however no matter what happens, make sure you implement this tactic and increase both your profits and customer satisfaction.

SUMMARY: THE MOST IMPORTANT LESSONS

I hope you noticed one recurring theme throughout this book: If you want to be successful....
You MUST be DIFFERENT in some way!
Right from the beginning of this book you read my success story which pointed out the importance of being DIFFERENT or adding a UNIQUE TWIST. This will NEVER change. This will ALWAYS be the difference between those who succeed and those who don't.

When I say different, people generally panic and think they can't come up with something new. I'm not talking about BIG difference here – You can build up on concepts that are already working by just doing something a little different.
The other important lesson is to maximize every marketing tactic at your disposal. For example, go

back and re-read that chapter about what Jimmy Brown is doing – It's brilliant!

Build a list. Introduce viral marketing. Introduce upselling. Introduce back-end selling.

Get the MOST out of what you've already got before moving onto another

project.

SUMMARY: DON'T FORGET THE SIMPLICITY OF IT ALL

Make sure you FOCUS on the simplicity of what you are trying to achieve.

Internet marketing sometimes can seem so confusing, however when you break it down into bite size steps you'll be amazed at its simplicity.

Your entire online business revolves around ONE thing - to make a sale...

To make this sale your whole business revolves around just TWO major tools...

Number 1

A direct response web site – I don't care if your web site consists of a thousand pages, each page must be designed to get the visitor to do something. Therefore, direct response.

Number 2

Collecting the email address of your visitors.

Everything else you do revolves around improving

the response rate to those two objectives.

I really want this to sink into your thinking! Really think about it...

Your web site is designed to make a sale. Inside of this part of the equation you will have to learn how to create a web site, how to write effective sales copy, how to accept payments, how to create thank you pages, how to rank high on search engines and how to get traffic to your web site and so on.

Capturing the email address of your visitor is designed so you can develop a relationship with your potential customers with the end-result to make a sale.

Inside this category you will need to learn about ecourses, newsletters, followup, pop-ups, subscription forms, and so on.

I'm really going to labor the point here...

Number 1 your web site - If you get one person to purchase your product from every 100 visitors you are doing well. Most sites may well be about one sale in 300 visitors or worse.

So, let's look at the best case-scenario and assume you get 1 sale from every 100 visitors.

That means that 99 out of hundred are gone forever, UNLESS you collect email addresses either by offering an ecourse or a newsletter.

Now you might get about 3 or maybe 5 of those 99 people to join your email list.

Then the chances are at least one of these will buy your product. Whammo - the little system has DOUBLED your sales.

But it gets better because as time goes by, the others who didn't purchase continue to get your newsletter which can result in them eventually buying or purchasing a product you recommend in your newsletter - thus you make more money.

Plus - people who already purchased from you continue to purchase the occasional product you recommend, further increasing your profits.

All because you have the simple, 2 step system in place.

And your whole marketing effort revolves around this system.

Can you increase your web site response to two sales every 100?

Can you increase sales from writing a better ecourse/newsletter?

I hope you see my point - EVERYTHING we discuss about web promotion will revolve around these two vital things.

And hopefully, after reading this article, it will have become obvious to you that Internet marketing isn't rocket science - it's doing the simple things right and then improving them.

Well, that's the end of Resale Rights Profits.

I sincerely hope that the information provided to you has helped you in two important areas.

1)To conquer the basics of setting up a resale rights business

2)To help ignite your creativity to be different and really profit from the resale rights business.
If this manual has helped you, I'd really like to hear about it.

We have Book Recommendations for you

The Strangest Secret by Earl Nightingale
(Audio CD - Jan 2006)

The Strangest Secret by Earl Nightingale
(Paperback)

Acres of Diamonds [MP3 AUDIO]
[UNABRIDGED] (Audio CD) by Russell H.
Conwell

Automatic Wealth: The Secrets of the Millionaire
Mind--Including: Acres of Diamonds, As a Man
Thinketh, I Dare you!, The Science of Getting
Rich, The Way to Wealth, and Think and Grow
Rich [UNABRIDGED]
by Napoleon Hill, et al (CD-ROM)

Think and Grow Rich [MP3 AUDIO]
[UNABRIDGED]
by Napoleon Hill, Jason McCoy (Narrator)
(Audio CD - January 30, 2006)

As a Man Thinketh [UNABRIDGED]
by James Allen, Jason McCoy (Narrator) (Audio
CD)

Your Invisible Power: How to Attain Your Desires
by Letting Your Subconscious Mind Work for You
[MP3 AUDIO] [UNABRIDGED]
by Genevieve Behrend, Jason McCoy (Narrator)
(Audio CD)

Thought Vibration or the Law of Attraction in the
Thought World [MP3 AUDIO] [UNABRIDGED]
by William Walker Atkinson, Jason McCoy
(Narrator) (Audio CD - July 1, 2005)

The Law of Success Volume I: The Principles of
Self-Mastery by Napoleon Hill (Audio CD - Feb
21, 2006)

The Law of Success, Volume I: The Principles of
Self-Mastery (Law of Success, Vol 1) (The Law of
Success) by Napoleon Hill (Paperback - Jun 20,
2006)

The Law of Success , Volume II & III: A Definite
Chief Aim & Self Confidence by Napoleon Hill
(Paperback - Jun 20, 2006)

Thought Vibration or the Law of Attraction in the
Thought World & Your Invisible Power
(Paperback)

Automatic Wealth, The Secrets of the Millionaire
Mind-Including: As a Man Thinketh, The Science
of Getting Rich, The Way to Wealth and Think
and Grow Rich (Paperback)

BN Publishing

Improving People's Life

www.bnpublishing.com

BN Publishing

Improving People's Life

www.bnpublishing.com